First Facts

Christmas around the World

Christmas in
GERMANY

by Jack Manning

CAPSTONE PRESS
a capstone imprint

First Facts are published by Capstone Press,
1710 Roe Crest Drive, North Mankato, Minnesota 56003
www.capstonepub.com

Library of Congress Cataloging-in-Publication Data
Manning, Jack.
  Christmas in Germany / by Jack Manning.
     pages cm.—(First facts: Christmas around the world)
  Includes index.
  ISBN 978-1-4765-3099-4 (library binding)
  ISBN 978-1-4765-3430-5 (ebook PDF)
1. Christmas—Germany—Juvenile literature. 2. Germany—Social life and customs—Juvenile
literature. I. Title.
  GT4987.49M36 2014
  394.26630943—dc23

                                                                            2013003258

Editorial Credits
Brenda Haugen, editor; Gene Bentdahl, designer; Eric Gohl, media researcher;
Jennifer Walker, production specialist

Photo Credits
AP Photo: Bernd Kammerer, cover; Capstone Studio: Karon Dubke, 21; Corbis: dpa/Matthias
Bein, 5; Newscom: Deutsch Presse Agentur/Stephan Jansen, 12, picture-alliance/dpa/Franziska
Kraufmann, 18, picture-alliance/dpa/Hendrik Schmidt, 7, picture-alliance/dpa/Robert Schlesinger,
15, picture-alliance/dpa/Soeren Stache, 11, Westend61 GmbH/hsimages, 16; Shutterstock: Jan S., 8,
LianeM, 1

Design Elements: Shutterstock

Printed in China by Nordica.
0314/CA21400180
022014   007226NORDF13

TABLE OF CONTENTS

Christmas in Germany

Music fills the cold winter air. People hang lights on houses. The smells of sweet treats drift from homes. It must be Christmas in Germany!

Germans celebrate Christmas Day on December 25. But they begin celebrating the Christmas season four weeks earlier. On January 6 the Christmas season ends. Germans call this day Three Kings' Day.

Germany

How to Say It!
In Germany people say *"Fröhliche Weihnachten"*
(FROH-lik-uh VEYE-nahkt-en), which means "Merry Christmas."

The First Christmas

Christians celebrate the birth of **Jesus** on Christmas. Mary was Jesus' mother. Joseph was Mary's husband. Long ago Mary and Joseph traveled to the Middle Eastern town of Bethlehem. The couple could not find a room where they could stay. They spent the night in a stable. Jesus was born there.

Three kings saw a bright star that led them to the baby Jesus. The kings brought gifts for Jesus.

CHRISTMAS FACT!

Jesus' first bed was a manger. A manger is a food box for animals.

Christian—a person who follows a religion based on the teachings of Jesus

Jesus—the founder of the Christian religion

Christmas Celebrations

Many people celebrate Christmas at Christmas markets. There they listen to music and watch puppet shows and plays. Shoppers buy food, toys, and decorations.

The Christmas tree is a big part of German celebrations. Parents spend Christmas Eve decorating the tree. When they hear a bell ring, the children come to see the decorated tree.

On Christmas Day many Germans go to church. They listen to the story of Jesus' birth. They also sing songs and listen to music.

Christmas Symbols

Germans were the first people to have Christmas trees. Many stories tell how **evergreen** trees became Christmas symbols. One story says Germans believed evergreen trees and lights kept away bad **spirits**. Germans put candles on the trees to protect themselves from bad spirits.

evergreen—a tree or bush that has green needles all year long
spirit—a ghost
clergyman—a minister or priest who carries on religious work

Another story tells about a German **clergyman** named Martin Luther. He walked in a forest one Christmas Eve. He thought the evergreens and stars were beautiful. Luther cut down an evergreen and put candles on it. He thought the candlelight looked like stars.

CHRISTMAS FACT!

An Advent wreath is a circle of greenery with four candles. Germans light one candle the first week of Christmas. They light two candles the second week. They light three the third week. Finally they light all four candles the fourth week.

Christmas Decorations

Christmas is a beautiful time in Germany. Strings of lights hang from houses, shops, and lampposts.

People decorate Christmas trees in many ways. Thin pieces of metal or paper called tinsel decorate many trees. Some people put candles, stars, or angels on their trees.

Germans decorate their homes with Advent calendars. The calendar runs from December 1 to Christmas Day.

Santa Claus

Who is that man with the white beard, red robe, pointed hat, and cane? Any German child can tell you that is Saint Nicholas! Children leave their shoes out for Saint Nicholas on December 5. The next day they find their shoes filled with toys and treats.

Some children write letters to the baby Jesus. They may ask for gifts. Some children put the letters on windowsills.

CHRISTMAS FACT!

Some children believe in the Weihnachtsmann (VEYE-nakts-mahn), which means "Christmas man." He looks like Saint Nicholas and brings gifts on Christmas Eve.

Christmas Presents

Presents remind Germans of the three kings' gifts to baby Jesus. Family members give one another presents on Christmas Eve. Some families read about Jesus' birth before opening presents.

Children may get dolls or trains. Some get jewelry, such as rings and necklaces. They also may receive clothes, books, or games.

Christmas Food

German homes are filled with wonderful smells at Christmas. Families eat many different foods during the Christmas season. Some eat roast goose or roast pork. Others eat turkey or duck. A fish called carp is another popular Christmas food.

Gingerbread is a popular treat in Germany. Some people use gingerbread as decorations. They make gingerbread cookies shaped like stars or bells. They hang the cookies on Christmas trees.

Gingerbread houses are popular too. Germans decorate the houses with frosting and candy.

CHRISTMAS FACT!

Marzipan (MAIR-zi-pan) is a popular Christmas treat. It is a candy made of ground almonds, egg whites, and sugar.

Christmas Songs

Have you ever heard the song "Oh Christmas Tree"? What about "Silent Night, Holy Night"? Or "Hark! The Herald Angels Sing"? All of these songs were written by Germans!

Christmas caroling is popular in Germany. Years ago poor Germans went from house to house. They sang outside each house. People sometimes gave the singers small gifts. Many Germans still enjoy Christmas caroling.

CHRISTMAS FACT!

Many German town bands play songs during the Christmas season. Bands play music in town squares. They also play songs in churches.

Hands-On:
MAKE A CHRISTMAS TREE

The Christmas tree is an important symbol in Germany. You can grow your own little Christmas tree at home!

What You Need
- one large pinecone
- one large bowl
- warm water
- one large pot
- soil
- grass seed
- scissors

What You Do
1. Remove any stem from the pinecone. This will help the cone stand up.
2. Fill the bowl with warm water. Soak the pinecone in the water for 10 minutes.
3. Put 1 inch (2.5 centimeters) of water in the pot. Remove the pinecone from the bowl, and put it in the pot.
4. Sprinkle soil onto the pinecone. Then sprinkle grass seed onto the pinecone. Put the pot in a sunny place.
5. Check your pinecone every day. Add water if the water level falls below 1 inch (2.5 cm).
6. Grass will grow on your pinecone. The pinecone will look like a Christmas tree. Trim the grass with a scissors when it becomes long.

GLOSSARY

Christian (KRIS-chuhn)—a person who follows a religion based on the teachings of Jesus

clergyman (KLUR-jee-man)—a minister or priest who carries on religious work

evergreen (E-vuhr-green)—a tree or bush that has green needles all year long

Jesus (JEE-zuhs)—the founder of the Christian religion

spirit (SPIHR-it)—a ghost

READ MORE

Hardyman, Robyn. *Celebrate Germany.* Celebrate!
New York: Chelsea Clubhouse, 2009.

Kelley, Emily. *Christmas around the World.* On My Own Holidays.
Minneapolis: Carolrhoda Books, 2004.

Trunkhill, Brenda. *Christmas Around the World.*
St. Louis: Concordia Publishing House, 2009.

INTERNET SITES

FactHound offers a safe, fun way to find Internet sites related
to this book. All of the sites on FactHound have been researched
by our staff.

Here's all you do:

Visit *www.facthound.com*

Type in this code: 9781476530994

Super-cool stuff!   Check out projects, games and lots more at
www.capstonekids.com

INDEX